21st Century
Junior Library

HOW DO THE THREE BRANCHES OF GOVERNMENT WORK TOGETHER?

Kevin Winn

T0001975

We the People:
U.S. Government at Work

Published in the United States of America by:

CHERRY LAKE PRESS
2395 South Huron Parkway, Suite 200, Ann Arbor, Michigan 48104
www.cherrylakepress.com

Reading Adviser: Beth Walker Gambro, MS, Ed., Reading Consultant, Yorkville, IL
Content Adviser: Mark Richards, Ph.D., Professor, Dept. of Political Science, Grand Valley State University, Allendale, MI

Photo Credits: cover: photo.ua/Shutterstock; page 5: © TREKPix/Shutterstock; page 6: U.S. Department of Defense; page 7: Ronald Reagan Presidential Library & Museum; page 8: Architect of the Capitol; page 9: Collection of the Supreme Court of the United States; page 11: Architect of the Capitol; page 12: Gerald R. Ford Library & Museum; page 14: Collection of the Supreme Court of the United States; page 16: Carol M. Highsmith/Library of Congress, Prints & Photographs Division; page 19: George Grantham Bain Collection/Library of Congress, Prints & Photographs Division; page 20: © Monkey Business Images/Shutterstock; page 21: © wavebreakmedia/Shutterstock

Copyright © 2023 by Cherry Lake Publishing Group

All rights reserved. No part of this book may be reproduced or utilized in any form or by any means without written permission from the publisher.

Cherry Lake Press is an imprint of Cherry Lake Publishing Group.

Library of Congress Cataloging-in-Publication Data

Names: Winn, Kevin P., author.
Title: How do the three branches of government work together? / Kevin Winn.
Description: Ann Arbor, Michigan : Cherry Lake Publishing, 2023. | Series: We the people: U.S. government at work | Includes index. | Audience: Grades 2-3
Summary: "Young readers will discover how the legislative, executive, and judicial branches work together and learn about the basic building blocks of the United States of America. They'll also learn about how they play a key role in American democracy. Series is aligned to 21st Century Skills curriculum standards. Engaging inquiry-based sidebars encourage students to Think, Create, Guess, and Ask Questions. Includes table of contents, glossary, index, author biography, and sidebars"– Provided by publisher.
Identifiers: LCCN 2022039596 | ISBN 9781668919415 (hardcover) | ISBN 9781668920435 (paperback) | ISBN 9781668921760 (ebook) | ISBN 9781668923092 (pdf)
Subjects: LCSH: United States–Politics and government–Juvenile literature. | Separation of powers–Juvenile literature.
Classification: LCC JK305 .W66 2023 | DDC 320.473–dc23/eng/20220915
LC record available at https://lccn.loc.gov/2022039596

Cherry Lake Press would like to acknowledge the work of the Partnership for 21st Century Learning, a Network of Battelle for Kids. Please visit http://www.battelleforkids.org/networks/p21 for more information.

Printed in the United States of America
Corporate Graphics

CHERRY LAKE PRESS

CONTENTS

THE UNITED STATES GOVERNMENT

In 1787, the Constitution of the United States was written. In 1788, it was ratified. The Constitution is the foundation of the U.S. government. On March 4, 1789, the U.S. federal government began.

The federal government has three branches. They are the executive branch, the legislative branch, and the judicial branch. Each branch has

GOVERNMENT

LEGISLATIVE

⬇

makes laws

EXECUTIVE

⬇

carries out laws

JUDICIAL

⬇

evaluates laws

The federal government has three branches.

important jobs. They work together to make sure no branch is too powerful. This is called checks and balances.

The executive branch is led by the president, the vice president, and the president's cabinet.

President George Bush sits with Marine generals.

President Ronald Reagan meets with his cabinet.

The president is also called the commander in chief. The commander in chief is the leader of the U.S. military. The president also makes sure the country follows Congress's laws.

The vice president has many important duties. The main and most important one is being ready. The vice president is next in line in case something happens to the president.

The cabinet is the vice president and a group of about 24 people the president chooses to lead sections of the government. They advise the president.

Congress is the legislative branch. Congress is made up of the Senate and the House of Representatives. Congress's main job is to make laws.

Vice presidents and presidents both swear to protect the U.S. Constitution.

The Senate has 100 members, two from each state. The House of Representatives has 435 members. Each state has at least one representative. States with a higher population have more representatives.

The third part of the government is the judicial branch, or the court system. The most powerful court is the Supreme Court. It has nine judges, or justices. Their job is to decide if laws follow the Constitution.

Think!

Presidents appoint Supreme Court justices. Justices serve for the rest of their lives. What are the positives of this? What are the negatives?

CHECKS AND BALANCES

The writers of the Constitution didn't want only one branch to rule the government. This would be too much like a **monarchy**—a type of government they were strongly against. Instead, the Constitution balances the powers among three branches. Using a system

President Richard Nixon resigned before Congress could impeach him.

of checks and balances, no single branch has total power.

How does this balance of power work? While the president holds the most powerful position, Congress must approve some presidential actions. For example, if the president chooses a new Supreme Court justice, Congress must approve the appointment.

One of Congress's most important powers is to **impeach**. Congress can impeach any member of the government, including the president. An official is impeached if they are charged with a crime or **misdemeanor**. If a majority of the House of Representatives votes to impeach, the Senate holds a trial. If found guilty, the person is removed from office.

Look!

The Supreme Court can affect laws. Sometimes a legal case can change a law. For instance, the *Brown v. Board of Education* case ended racial segregation in schools. The Supreme Court ruled that racial segregation was against the Fourteenth Amendment to the U.S. Constitution. Research this amendment. How did racial segregation violate this amendment? Research other amendments. Can you think of other rulings or laws that go against the Constitution? Discuss your ideas with a friend or family member.

Supreme Court Justices determine if laws are constitutional.

Congress's power is checked by both the Supreme Court and the president. If Congress approves a **bill**, the president can **veto** it. This means the bill does not become a law.

Supreme Court justices can also disagree with Congress if they believe a law goes against the Constitution. This helps keep Congress from becoming too powerful.

Make a Guess!

The president receives many bills. The president signs some and vetoes others. The president has 10 days to do this. Why do you think there is a time limit?

OUR GOVERNMENT TODAY

The three branches of the U.S. government have changed since 1787. These include adding amendments to the Constitution. The first 10 amendments are called the Bill of Rights. These went into effect in 1791.

Since 1791, there have been plenty of suggested amendments. But only 17 more amendments have been passed. All the amendments are important.

A very important one is the Thirteenth Amendment. This amendment made slavery illegal.

Amending the Constitution is a complicated process. But with enough support, change can happen. The Thirteenth Amendment was supported by many activists. They fought for the rights of all people.

The government holds important power. But the role of the government is to work for and serve its citizens. By voting in elections and fighting inequities, people keep elected officials in check. That's an additional check and balance.

Ask Questions!

The U.S. Constitution has 27 amendments. Pick one of the amendments and find out more about it. Why was it added to the Constitution? Who does the amendment affect?

ACTIVITY

Get inspired! Choose one activist to research. Examples include Ida B. Wells and Frances Ellen Watkins Harper. Others are Greta Thunberg and Malala Yousafzai. How do they inspire others? How do they inspire you? Tell your family about the activist and what they stood for.

GLOSSARY

activists (AK-tih-vists) people who work on social issues

amendments (uh-MEND-muhnts) additions or changes to the Constitution

appointment (uh-POYNT-muhnt) position or office to which a person is named

bill (BIL) draft of a law

cabinet (KAB-nit) group of people who advise the U.S. president

constitution (kahn-stuh-TOO-shuhn) set of rules that guides a country

federal (FEH-duh-ruhl) relating to the national level of U.S. government

impeach (im-PEECH) charge a government official with a crime or misdemeanor

inequities (ih-NEH-kwuh-teez) things that are not fair

misdemeanor (mis-dih-MEE-nuhr) small crime

monarchy (MAH-nuhr-kee) government led by a king or queen

ratified (RAH-tuh-fyed) made valid or effective; gave legal approval

segregation (seh-gruh-GAY-shuhn) act of separating one group of people from another based on things such as race, gender, or religion

veto (VEE-toh) strike down or go against

violate (VYE-uh-layt) to go against or disregard

FIND OUT MORE

Books

Baxter, Roberta. *The Creation of the U.S. Constitution.* Ann Arbor, MI: Cherry Lake Publishing, 2014.

Bedesky, Baron. *What is a Government?* New York, NY: Crabtree Publishing Co., 2008.

Cheney, Lynne. *We the People.* New York, NY: Simon & Schuster, 2012.

Christelow, Eileen. *Vote!* New York, NY: Clarion Books, 2018.

Taylor-Butler, Christine. *The Congress of the United States.* New York, NY: Scholastic, 2008.

Websites

Ben's Guide to the U.S. Government
https://bensguide.gpo.gov
Let Ben Franklin guide you through the whos and whats of our government.

iCivics
https://icivics.org
Find out how you can be an informed and involved citizen.

INDEX

ABOUT THE AUTHOR

Kevin Winn is a children's book writer and researcher. He focuses on issues of racial justice and educational equity in his work. In 2020, Kevin earned his doctorate in Educational Policy and Evaluation from Arizona State University.